GROWING IN FAITH

Steve Clark

SERVANT BOOKS
Ann Arbor, Michigan

Published by: Servant Books
              Box 8617
              Ann Arbor, Michigan 48107

Available from: Servant Publications
                 Distribution Center
                 237 North Michigan
                 South Bend, Indiana 46601

Scripture taken from **Today's English Version** and the **Revised Standard Version**. Used with permission.

ISBN 0-89283-004-2

INTRODUCTION

"Didn't I tell you that if you would have faith, you would see God's glory?" These were Jesus' words to Martha just before raising Lazarus from the dead. And Martha did see the glory of God when Lazarus walked out from the tomb. God is glorified when he works in a powerful way that men can see and appreciate. When Jesus healed people, cast out demons from them, and even raised them from the dead, men saw God's glory before their eyes in a way that they could not easily miss. And the glory of God is what we are looking for when we want the life of the Spirit. We want a life which is lived by the power of God, a life in which God is at work in a way that can be experienced and seen. We want to see the glory of God in our own lives, and we want God to be glorified among men.

The key to seeing the glory of God is illustrated in the story of Lazarus. Jesus had heard that Lazarus was sick, close to death. He deliberately waited until Lazarus had died, and then came to Bethany, the home of Lazarus and his sisters, Mary and Martha. Once there, he went to the tomb:

> "Deeply moved once more, Jesus went to the tomb, which was a cave with a stone placed at the entrance. 'Take the stone away!' Jesus ordered. Martha, the dead man's sister, answered. 'There will be a bad smell, Lord. He has been buried four days!' Jesus said to her, 'Didn't I tell you that if you would have faith (believed), you would see God's glory?' They took the stone away, Jesus looked up and said: 'I thank you, Father, that you listen to me. I know that you always listen to me, but I say this because of the people here, so they will believe that you sent me.' After he had

said this he called out in a loud voice, 'Laz-
arus, come out!' The dead man came out with
his hands and feet wrapped in grave cloths,
and a cloth around his face. 'Untie him,'
Jesus told them, 'and let him go.' "

(John 11:38-44)

The key to seeing the glory of God, the key to experiencing the life of the Spirit, the key to having God work in us and through us powerfully is faith. If we have faith, we will see things happen that are beyond human power. If we have faith, we will see God work in ways that we had not hoped for.

Sometimes we think that faith is only needed for beginning the Christian life, for getting into a relationship with the Lord. Faith is for the beginning of our Christian life, but it is also meant to be a part of our lives as Christians all the way through. Saint Paul says:

"As therefore you received Christ Jesus the
Lord, so live in him, rooted and built up in
him and established in the faith, just as you
were taught, abounding in thanksgiving."

(Col. 2:6,7)

Whenever we want to see God do something, whenever we want to experience his presence or see him improve a situation, we need faith. If we want to live the life of the Spirit, we have to live the life of faith. Faith makes it possible for the Holy Spirit to live in us and work through us.

God Wants
To Do It

Often, all too often, our attitude towards God is more like the attitude of a Stoic than of a Christian. A Stoic's attitude is, "Whatever happens is the will of God. Therefore, I'll just wait and see what God does to me, and whatever it turns out to be is the best thing possible." Sometimes devout Christians say it this way: "What I want most is what God wants. Therefore, whatever God does is fine with me."

It is true, we should want above all what God wants. If we love him, we should want to please him. But if we fall into a Stoic attitude of accepting the things that happen to us as God's will, then we have missed two important Christian truths. We have missed, first of all, the truth that God has already told us what he wants. He has shown us what pleases him and what he wants to do. Therefore, by what he has said to us we can tell that many things that happen to us are not his will; sometimes they are even the result of what Satan has been trying to do. We can also tell that there are things that should be happening with us that are not happening.

We have also missed the important Christian truth that God wants us to ask things from him, even to demand the things from him that we need or that he has promised us. He does not want passive, quietly resigned children. He wants eager children who want to know him, who want to experience his presence, who want to see his glory. Jesus himself said this to us through a story in the eleventh chapter of Luke,

"And Jesus said to his disciples: 'Suppose one of you should go to a friend's house at midnight and tell him, 'Friend, let me bor-

row three loaves of bread. A friend of mine who is on a trip has just come to my house and I don't have a thing to offer him!' And suppose your friend should answer from inside, 'Don't bother me! The door is already locked, my children and I are in bed, and I can't get up to give you anything.' Well, what then? I tell you, even if he will not get up to give you the bread because he is your friend, yet he will get up and give you everything you need because you are not ashamed to keep on asking. And so I say to you: Ask, and you will receive; seek and you will find; knock, and the door will be opened to you.' "

(Luke 11:5-9)

God does not want us to be passively waiting for him to do his will, but he wants us to be asking, seeking, knocking. He wants to have us hungry to see his glory. It is only when we are anxious to know him and to see him change us and to see him do things in the world that we are ready to have faith.

Faith is based upon the knowledge that God wants to do things for us and through us; he has told us that he wants to do things for us, and for that reason we can have faith that he will. The

Scripture is filled with God's promises, his stated intentions of what he wants to do for us and through us. For instance, in the fifth chapter of John's first letter (1 John 5:3,4), it says "His commands are not too hard for us, for every child of God is able to defeat the world. This is how we win the victory over the world; with our faith." A verse in the previous chapter (1 John 4:4) reads: "He who is in you is greater than he who is in the world." We have confidence that we can keep God's commandments and overcome the world because God is living in us, and he is able. Another promise is found in John's Gospel (John 14:12) where Jesus says to his disciples, "I tell you the truth: whoever believes in me will do the works I do—yes, he will do even greater ones, for I am going to the Father." There is a simple fact at the basis of our faith—God wants to work in us and through us and he can do anything he wants.

Not only does God want to work in us and through us, but he wants to do more than we usually look for him to do. A few years ago a friend of mine and I were traveling on the West Coast. We had gone out for a conference on evangelism, but one of our main interests was to visit some people we had heard about who seemed to know a great deal about faith and spiritual gifts. These people invited us to go to a Kathryn Kuhlman service. Kathryn Kuhlman calls herself an evangelist, but most people would describe her as a healer. Once a month she holds services in the Shrine Auditorium in Los Angeles. The Shrine Auditorium holds about 7,000 people, and when Kathryn Kuhlman comes, it is filled to capacity. People are turned away at the doors.

The meeting we went to began with praise and worship—7,000 people in a huge auditorium glorifying God. Just that itself impressed me. Then part way through the service, she called some people who had been there the month before onto the stage to share what had happened to them. One man had had arthritis so bad that, as he put it over and over again, "I couldn't even weed my garden." In the course of the meeting he had first come to, while he was sitting in a back room in which he could not even see the service, he had been totally healed. A second man had come to the service only because a friend had insisted on it. He did not believe in Christ and had no expectation that he would be healed of the terminal cancer from which he was suffering. Toward the end of the service, he felt something like a rush of water go through him, and afterwards, he felt much better. The following week he visited his doctor who certified that he had been healed and even brought the X-rays to the service to show everyone.

After the two testimonies the service turned to prayer again, and then, all of a sudden, Kathryn Kuhlman said something like: "Up there in that balcony somebody is being healed of arthritis," and then, "Somebody down there can walk now and if he will throw away his crutches, he will find that it is so." She pointed out a number of other people in the audience who were being healed. And I thought to myself, "that sounds good." But then people started coming up to the stage, and they told about the different things that had happened to them. One was cured of arthritis (a number of people in fact had been cured of arthritis that night), someone came up with his crutches to report on his cure, a boy deaf in one ear could hear with it. Dozens of people came forward with impressive healings.

One of the cases I found most impressive was a woman who had had to wear braces over her whole body and had walked on crutches. I had just happened to see her and talk to her before the meeting. As the different people were coming forward, I saw a man carrying all the braces and gear the crippled woman had been wearing, while she herself was walking in front. She told the people of how she had had an automobile accident about five or six years before, and since then had had a number of operations, some of which had helped a little, but no doctor could cure her. And yet here she was in front of us bending and jumping and walking back and forth.

I found that service a great experience for improving my faith. It showed me that the Lord not only could do things like that; he actually did them in front of me. About a month later when we were back home, a minister from the East Coast, the father of one of our friends, came to visit us. He told us the story of how one time he had worked with Kathryn Kuhlman in her service, and afterwards, for the help he had given her, she gave him a copy of her book, *I Believe in Miracles.* The inscription in it was: "There's more, so much more."

My reaction at that time was that if I could only have as much of God's working as I had seen at the Kuhlman service I would be satisfied. There is a tendency in me to rest with what I have, to feel that this is enough. Since I have already gotten more from the Christian life than I had expected, I am tempted to just sit back and enjoy it. But Kathryn Kuhlman was expressing an attitude of the Christian life that we all need to have: that God has more for us and that we should desire it and expect it from him. If we put an upper limit on what the Lord is going to do for us, or if we say that we have had enough, God has a harder time doing what he wants to do for us.

The life of faith begins when we have our eyes opened to a truth: the truth that the all-powerful Creator of everything is with us and wants to do things for us and through us. His power is available, and he is ready to do a great deal, in fact a great deal more than we are hoping for. We are in the position of Elisha's servant:

> "When the servant of the man of God rose early in the morning, an army with horses and chariots was surrounding the city. And the servant said, 'Alas, my master! What shall we do?' He said, 'Don't be afraid, for those who are with us are more than those who are with them.' Then Elisha prayed, and said, 'O Lord, open his eyes that he may see.' So the Lord opened the eyes of the young man, and he saw; and behold, the mountain was full of horses and chariots of fire round about Elisha."

(2 Kings 6:15-17)

We are surrounded by the power of God, by armies of angels and saints, and once we see that, once we see that we do not have to depend on our own personal resources to live the Christian life, we are on the way to living the life of faith.

Faith is simply the way to tap the spiritual power which is available to us. At this moment, there are all kinds of power in the room we are in. There are magnetic waves, radio waves, even nuclear power. Two thousand years ago, the same power was on the earth, but people did not know how to tap it. Since then, we have learned how to make contact with that power so that we can have electric lights or can hear music that is playing hundreds of miles away. But in the same room, there is even greater spiritual power than there is physical power. The power of God is with us right now. We need to learn how to tap that power, we need to learn how to have faith.

Now for some people it seems unfair that God should make faith the way to tap his power. They feel that it is as difficult to have faith as it was for people two thousand years ago to hear music that was being played four hundred miles away. They feel that God is just trying to make it hard for them, that he is trying to set up an insurmountable obstacle to their receiving his gifts. Faith seems as out of reach as miracles do. And yet the Lord is not asking for faith because he wants to make the

Christian life hard for us. He is asking for faith, because his intention is to make the Christian life easy for us. Or perhaps a better way of saying it is, he is asking for faith because he wants to make it possible for us to do more and to see more happen than we ever thought was possible. Faith is what he is asking for because faith is simply the way we let him do things in us and through us. Faith is a way of yielding to God so that he can do things through us.

Perhaps a brief analogy will help illustrate how faith is a key to letting God work in our lives. Suppose we took someone who did not know how to swim, a person who had not yet experienced how it was possible to stay afloat and move through water; if we were to throw him into a lake, odds are that he would struggle so hard to stay up that he would not be able to stay up at all. He would be so afraid that "it wouldn't work" (after all, everyone knows that bodies are heavier than water), that he would thrash around until he went under. But if we can give him faith first, if we can give him faith in the buoyant power of the water, he can easily stay afloat. His faith in the buoyant power of the water will let him relax so that he can allow the water to hold him up. Then he will be able to move around in the water and learn to swim.

We need the same kind of faith to live the life of the Spirit. The power of God is there to hold us up and to let us move in ways we did not think possible. When we struggle the hardest to stay up or to get results, we have the hardest time. What we do when we struggle that way is to act as though the only way we can make progress is by our own power. But when we learn how to trust the Spirit in us, when we learn how to relax and let God do with his power what he wants to do in us and through us, then things begin to happen.

Faith makes it possible for us to count on and cooperate with what God is doing. Let us say that we want to get into a locked closet. If someone were to come to us, hand us a key and say "that is the key to the closet," it would be a simple matter for us to take the key and use it to open the door. Even if we encountered some difficulty in getting the key into the lock the first time we tried, we would not give up. We would approach the situation as if we had the key—and we would be able to unlock the door. We have been given the Holy Spirit as the key to living the Christian life. We need only to approach the Christian life as if we had the key. We need only have faith in the Holy Spirit living in us. If we do that, then we are able to see his work in us; we are able to count on it and cooperate with it.

We have to know and believe a simple fact before the life of faith is possible: that God wants to do things for us and through us. Once we know he wants to, we know that the power from God is available, then we will be able to rely on it, expect it, and act on it.

What Is Faith?

Many times the reason people feel they are unable to have faith is that they misunderstand what faith is. Often people think of faith as a blind leap. According to this view faith consists in deciding to believe that something will happen even though there is no good reason to do so. Faith is seen simply as a blind act of the will, a leap with no assurance that there is a landing place. There are times in life when it is worth taking a blind leap (sometimes we have no alternative), but

Christian faith, the faith which the Lord Jesus spoke about, is not the same thing as taking a blind leap.

In the letter to the Hebrews, faith is described in the following way:

> "To have faith is to be sure of the things we hope for, to be certain of the things we cannot see."

(Heb. 11:1)

Although we do not see the things we are having faith for (if we saw it we would have knowledge of it, not faith for it), yet faith gives us a sureness, a certainty. We can have faith because we know something that allows us to expect that God will do certain things. Christian faith is a faith in the unseen, but it is not blind. A Christian does not have faith when he is in darkness, but when he has seen a light, and that light is God's revelation to us.

Sometimes a Christian has caught only a glimpse of that light. Sometimes he can see only dimly (and therefore makes mistakes). But still he sees a light. Faith is a response to the fact that God is there, and that he has shown us what we can expect from him. Once we know the truth, once we see (or begin to see) by the light of revelation, we can have faith. Faith is expecting God to do what he has shown us he will do—expecting it, counting on it, and doing those things which allow him to do what he has shown us he wants to do.

There are many ways that God reveals to us what he wants to do. God reveals what he wants to do through a promise that we know always holds. Then our faith can be sure no matter what the situation. Once we know that God has said he always wants something to happen, then we can simply count on it and expect it to happen. We can find promises like this in Scripture. One such promise is the promise Christ made in the eleventh chapter of Luke when he said that the Father would give the Holy Spirit to those who would ask him for it:

> *"Everyone who asks will receive, and he who seeks will find, and the door will be opened to him who knocks. Would any one of you fathers give his son a snake when he asks for a fish? Or would you give him a scorpion when he asks for an egg? As stingy as you are, you know how to give good things to your children. How much more, then, the Father in heaven will give the Holy Spirit to those who ask him!"*

> (Luke 11:10-13)

After I was prayed with to be baptized in the Spirit at Duquesne, I had difficulty for a while in opening up to the life of the Spirit. One of the big questions for me then was, would "it" happen to me or not? It happened to so-and-so and it happened to so-and-so, but would it ever happen to me? Would I ever get baptized in the Spirit? I was not clear on what "it" was, and since I had not experienced anything very distinctive when I was prayed with, I was not sure anything had happened. Therefore, I was not sure whether I could experience any of the things the Spirit was supposed to do for people — tongues, guidance, or anything else. I felt a great uncertainty, and therefore my whole Christian life began to lose confidence.

At some point, I began to understand things differently. I could see that according to the Scripture, the Holy Spirit is for everyone. If you are a Christian, you can have the gift of the Spirit if you ask for it. That is what the Lord promised in Luke 11. In fact, he said that the Father was generous in giving the Holy Spirit. He was eager for people to have the Holy Spirit at work in their lives. Christ seemed to say that the promise held true regardless of the situation. Therefore, since I had asked, I could count on having received it.

My new understanding made things very different. Once I began to proceed on the basis that Christ's promise was reliable, all of a sudden things began to happen. I soon yielded to tongues, began to experience the Spirit guiding me, and began to experience some of his power in prayer. Or rather, to be more accurate, I did not so much yield to tongues as come to discover that the Holy Spirit had been prompting me to speak in tongues all along, and that I had not really had faith in it. I did not so much begin to experience the Holy Spirit guiding me; rather, I began to recognize the guidance he had already been giving me. It was not so much that God did something new for me; rather, I began to have faith in the promise God had made. I began to experience things happening to me that the Scriptures said were supposed to happen.

There are promises the Lord has made that we can count on. Whenever the Lord says that something will happen if something else is done ("you will be given the Holy Spirit if you ask for it"), then we know we can count on that happening if we meet the conditions, even if it remains unseen for a while. Whenever the Lord gives a command ("rejoice always"), or describes the Christian life ("love is patient and kind"), then we know we can expect those things to happen to us as we grow as Christians. We know that regardless of the situation, we should expect all the things that are part of the Christian life to happen to us.

There are, however, many things that the Lord would like to do (and that we need faith for) that are not covered by universal promises. Therefore, we cannot appeal to Scripture to know for certain that we can see them happen. Maybe we want healing. Maybe we need some money. Maybe we would like things to work out so that somebody can hear about the Lord. We know the Lord heals people, that he provides for his people's needs and that he wants people to hear about him. But we cannot always be sure that in this particular situation he will heal, provide money, or arrange circumstances. There are many such things that come our way, but when we look through the Scriptures we cannot exactly find a promise that will guarantee that we can expect these things to happen.

The Lord has another way of revealing to us what he is ready to do. As we grow in the life of the Spirit, the Lord begins to speak to us and lead us. Sometimes his direction comes to us as an inner word. Sometimes it is just an inner sense, a witness to our own spirit. We come to know in a spiritual way that all we have to do is ask for something and it will happen or all we will have to do is act in a certain way so that the Lord can work through us and a certain result will happen. We get directly from God a spiritual assurance.

A short while back, I was speaking to a student who was not a Christian. He had come back from summer vacation with some serious difficulties. During the summer he had faced the apparent meaninglessness of his own life and he was anxious about what he saw. He had come to me because we had known one another before and he was wondering if God was the answer. While I was talking with him I began to get a sense, a quiet sense, that the Lord wanted to help him to see the Lord had the power to do things for him. The thought came to my mind, and I sensed that I could pray for him and he would experience a healing; that he would experience his anxiety go away and would experience himself being freed from some of the things that were bothering him.

So I put faith in what God was showing me. I talked to him for a while, and then I said, "I can pray for you. God has given me the power to pray for you, and when I do, you will experience a change. There will be a new peace afterwards." He was willing to try anything, so we prayed together, and as I prayed the Lord led me in the prayer. I felt that I should pray for the healing of some specific things that had happened to him in the past. As I was praying for one specific situation, I had a mental image of Christ touching a red sore spot and then of black matter flowing out. Just as soon as that happened, he started to cry and he began to talk about the situation I had prayed for. It was a purging experience for him, and when it was over, he said that he had not realized how much that situation had bothered him. By the time we were done, there had been a healing. God had done the very thing that I had promised he would do.

We cannot always expect God to work this way. After all, many times when we want to ask God for a healing, healing is not the thing which is needed. But when I was in that situation, I had a sense that God was willing to do it for him. In other words, God revealed to me something that he would do. My part was to have faith in that revelation — to believe that it was actually from God, to rely on it, and then to do what I had to do; to make a promise to him on God's behalf and then to pray for him so that the promise would come true. And it did.

There is yet a third way we can have faith through God's revelation. Sometimes we do not have a universal promise that we can count on, nor do we have some sort of direct leading or word from the Lord about this particular situation, and yet it is still right to have faith in the situation. We may not have as much assurance as we would like, but we can still step out and have confidence in the Lord. We do so simply because God has revealed to us that he loves us and that he likes to do good things for his children.

A few months ago a friend came to visit me and stayed overnight. When we got up for morning prayers and breakfast, I noticed that he was limping. One foot seemed to have some kind of pain in it, and he could not walk on it very well. After breakfast, we all prayed together, and while we were praying the thought came to mind—the obvious Christian thought—perhaps we should pray for his foot to be healed. The Lord heals people, and Christians have the power to pray for such healings. There was a certain reluctance for me to pray for it, but I decided that if I believed in Christ, I really ought to. So I suggested to him that we pray for the foot to be healed, and he agreed. I laid hands on him and we prayed for the healing. Then we went back to morning prayers, and after we had finished praying, I asked him, "How's your foot?" He said with a surprised look on his face, "The pain's gone. It's healed." And then I said with an even more surprised look on my face, "It is healed?"

Now it is fairly obvious that his foot was not healed because we were filled with a great feeling of faith. Nor had I felt any special indication from the Lord that he wanted to heal the foot. Moreover I do not believe that there is any promise in Scripture that the Lord will always and everywhere heal everything. But on the other hand, I know that the Lord has promised that he will heal, and I know that he likes to give those who believe in him what they ask for. I was able to put enough faith in the Lord to pray for the healing, and it happened.

We can also have faith even when we do not receive an inner revelation from God or have a specific promise from Scripture about a situation; we can do this because we know what God is like. We know that he has power and that he wants to work through us. We can make that the basis of our "leap." In other words, God wants us to develop an overall attitude of faith in him. He wants us to expect him to do more and more — even when we cannot find a specific promise that covers it or when we have no specific leading for it. As we have more and more faith in him, we will see more and more happening.

Faith, then, is not a blind leap, but it is a response to revelation. It is a response to what we know of God and what he wants to do. But it is a very particular kind of response.

Faith is the response we make to a rock. A rock can be relied upon. A man can lean upon a rock, or build upon a rock. He cannot trust sand, but he can trust rock. Because it is firm, he can count upon it and expect things from it.

In the Psalms, the Lord is called our rock. He is our rock, because we can rely upon him. When he says something, we can count upon it. If he indicates to us something will happen, we can expect it. If he tells us to do something, we should act upon it. We know, because he is trustworthy, that we have a firm footing when we walk in faith in him.

There are three kinds of faith — believing faith, trusting faith, and expecting faith — and we do not begin to see the glory of God until we have expecting faith. Believing faith could also be called doctrinal faith. Many people have this kind of faith because they accept the Christian truths. They have faith that Christ is the Son of God or that there is a heaven and a hell. Trusting faith is faith in God's goodness. When people have trusting faith, they believe that everything will turn out well. God will take care of them because he loves them. Believing faith and trusting faith are both important, but they are not enough to see God's glory.

The difference between just having believing faith or trusting faith and having expectant faith can be seen in the story of the woman suffering from severe bleeding that is told in Mark's Gospel:

"Then Jesus started off. So many people were going along with him that they were crowding him from every side. There was a woman who had suffered terribly from severe bleeding for twelve years, even though she had been treated by many doctors. She had spent all her money, but instead of getting better, she got worse all the time. She had heard about Jesus, so she came in the crowd behind him. 'If I touch just his clothes,' she said to herself, 'I shall get well.' She touched his cloak and her bleeding stopped at once; and she had the feeling inside herself that she was cured of her trouble. At once Jesus felt that power had gone out of him. So he turned around in the crowd and said, 'Who touched my clothes?' His disciples answered, 'You see that people are crowding you; why do you ask who touched you' But Jesus kept looking around

*to see who had done it. The woman realized
what had happened to her; so she came, trem-
bling with fear, and fell at his feet and told
him the whole truth. Jesus said to her, 'My
daughter, your faith has made you well, Go in
peace, and be healed from your trouble.' "*

(Mark 5:24-34)

As Jesus was walking through the crowds, the
woman suffering from severe bleeding came up to
him. She reached out to touch him, and when she
did, she was healed. It was her faith that allowed
her to be healed. But it was not just believing faith
that she had. When she reached out to touch him
she did not say, "This man is the Son of God," or,
"this man is the Messiah, and I want to touch
him." She might not even have known who he was.
All she knew was that he had healed people. Nor
was it just trusting faith that she had. When she
reached out to him, she did not say, "This is a
good man, a man I can trust. He will see that whatever happens to me is the best possible thing."
Rather, she had expectant faith. She said, "If I
touch just his clothes, I shall get well." She did not
just believe in who Jesus was, nor did she just trust
him, but she expected that if she touched him, she
would be healed. She reached out to him in expectant faith, and that, Jesus said, is what healed her.

The kind of faith which makes it possible for us to see the glory of God is expectant faith. God wants us to reach out for many things, because we have a confident expectation that he will do things for us if we only turn to him. When we put that kind of faith in him, things happen.

Expectant faith often means that we have to do something before we see God act. A good example of the active element in our faith is Peter's walking on the water. Peter saw Christ walking across the lake, coming closer to them. When Peter saw him, he asked Christ to let him walk on the water. So Christ told him to come, and he did. He stepped out of the boat and began to walk.

In order for Peter to walk on water, he actually had to walk. It may sound stupid to say it that way, but Peter's part was to walk, and his part was indispensable. There would be no walking on water unless Peter actually did some walking. It was the power of Christ which made it possible for the water to hold Peter up, but the power of Christ could not do everything. His power could be there, but if Peter had never stepped out of the boat and walked, there would have been no story to tell.

In order to walk on the water, Peter needed some expectant faith. He may not have needed a lot, but he at least needed enough to take the necessary step. Moreover, he not only had to expect something to happen. He also had to do something to make it possible. His expectant faith had to lead to action. He had to act upon what he knew Christ had said.

What is faith, then? Faith is a response to God's revelation. Once God begins to show us something about what we can expect from him, we need to respond to that by believing it, counting on it, acting upon it. As we begin to put expectant faith in what God is showing us we begin to see things happen.

GROWING IN FAITH

Ten years ago, if people had told me that I would pray with someone to receive the gift of tongues, and he would receive it, I would have thought that they were not quite in touch with reality. Not only did my faith in the area not reach very far. It was almost nonexistent. And yet now, I expect it all the time. In fact, if I were to prepare someone and then pray with him and he did not receive the gift of tongues, I would wonder why not.

The Lord has made many changes in me. He has built up my faith far beyond what it used to be. I expect him to do more and more. In many areas of my life, my faith in God is unquestioning. When I notice lacks in me in the area of the fruit of the Spirit and pray for the Lord to make a change, I fully expect to see progress begin soon. On the other hand, there are other areas where my faith is lower. If I pray for someone and he is healed, I am not surprised, the way I would have been ten years ago; but on the other hand, my faith in that area is not as great as it is when I pray with someone for the gift of tongues. Moreover, I must confess, I would be surprised if I prayed with someone who was dead and he got up. But then again, I would not be surprised to see the Lord building my faith in that area so that I might expect to see it happen some day.

Faith grows. We do not have to be upset when we notice that we do not yet have faith to move mountains. Often when people have been baptized in the Spirit, they begin to feel nervous and guilty about the way they exercise faith. They read the promises Christ made to those who have faith, and they think they should be able to do all those things at once. Sometimes they even become fearful of trying anything, because they think it might not happen and they fear that that might prove fatal to what little faith they think they have. Or they do try praying for some thing and it does not happen, and then they start feeling guilty about how little faith they have.

What the Lord expects from us is not mature, fully formed faith all at once (of most of us anyway), but the readiness to grow in faith. Even more, he wants us to have an expectance to grow in faith. He does not want us to be anxious about the shortcomings in our faith but he wants us to look to him and expect him to build faith in us. In other words, he wants us to know that faith comes from him and that it grows. As we expect him to build our faith, we will begin to see changes.

Often God builds our faith through experiences. Our faith is fed when we see God act. After I saw the Kathryn Kuhlman service I described above, my faith was different. In fact it has never been quite the same since. Because I saw what God **could** do, I found it easier to believe in what he **would** do. As I see him doing more things around me in a daily way, I find faith easier and easier. Almost without thinking about it, I have come to expect God to do many things as a matter of course that ten years ago I would have been very excited about. Just today, some friends shared with me some sudden changes in their lives that had come through prayer. I was happy that the changes had happened, but I did not think twice about the way they had happened. I have come to expect that God will work in that way.

God also builds our faith through people who have faith. If we live with Christians who have faith, we will find faith growing in us. If we live with Christians who are fearful and who have little faith, or if we live with little personal contact with other committed Christians, we will find ourselves struggling to keep our faith alive.

Recently the Lord began to speak to our community about having more faith. He told us that we did not count on his promises enough, that we often reacted to situations as if he were not there or would not help us, that we often acted like a group of orphans. That word from the Lord changed us, and our whole community began to pray for healings of all sorts, began to ask him to supply things they needed but could not find or afford, began to ask him to fix machines that were not working, to find things that were missing. Not only did the community begin to pray more for big things, but they also prayed for little things. They tried to meet each situation more consistently in faith.

As those around me began to change, I began to notice something happening to me. I found myself having more faith and expecting the Lord to do more all the time. The change did not come because I took some special steps. It was more because the faith of others "rubbed off." It felt like I was catching faith from others. And I believe the Lord wants it to be that way. He wants us to have our faith built up by other members of his Body.

The Lord often builds faith in us by directly imparting it to us spiritually. When we are baptized in the Spirit the Lord imparts faith. Many times he imparts faith as we pray. We experience the Lord's presence in a strong way or we hear him speak to us in a clear way, and afterwards we find that we have more faith. The more we come to know the Lord and the more we experience his reality, the more faith we find that we have.

Although faith grows in us because of what God does to us, we do have a part in the growth of our faith. We can cooperate with him as he works to increase our faith. If we learn some simple lessons, we will find ourselves growing steadily in faith.

LISTEN TO GOD'S WORD

In order for us to grow in faith, we have to hear God speak to us. The words he speaks to us build faith in us. He speaks a message to us that frees us to have faith. Paul explains it this way,

> "The Scripture says, 'Whoever believes in him will not be disappointed'. This includes everyone, for God is the Lord of all and richly blesses all who call on him. As the Scripture says, 'Everyone who calls upon the name of the Lord will be saved.' But how can they call on him, if they have not believed? And how can they believe if they have not heard the message? And how can they hear, if the message is not preached? And how can the message be preached, if the messengers are not sent out? . . . So then, faith comes from hearing the message, and the message comes through preaching Christ."

(Rom. 10:11-17)

It is hearing the basic Christian truths presented to us that allows us to have the kind of faith we need.

God's word comes to us in many ways. The most important way is through the Scriptures, and therefore if we want to grow in faith, we should read the Scriptures regularly. But it also comes through prophecy, through words that other Christians speak to us that are prompted by the Spirit and through words that God speaks to us directly as we learn how to listen for his voice. God's word is alive, and that means that he wants to speak to us constantly. Moreover, usually it turns out that the things he wants to say to us are the same simple things: faith-building truths.

The truths that build faith the most quickly are usually the most basic truths. For instance, one of the most faith-building truths is that God loves us. He created us because he loves us and he wants us in existence because he loves us. He became man and died on a cross for us because he loves us. His care and concern for us is constant, because he loves us. No matter what situation we are in, we can know that we can count on his love. As we grow in consciousness of the truth that he is a loving Father, we can pray and act in faith more easily. We know in every situation that we can count on him to be for us.

A second faith-building truth is that the Lord is with us. He does not leave us, but he is there with us. That means that whatever situation we are facing, whatever concern we are wondering about, the Lord is there with us. We do not have to act in any situation as if we were alone. We can always expect the Lord to be there and to make his help available. Much of our lack of faith comes simply from our forgetfulness of the Lord.

A third faith-building truth is that Christ is in us through the power of his Spirit. Not only is he with us in every situation, he is in us. That means that we can count on him to act through us, to give us the strength that we need, to supply us with wisdom, to even give us faith. Paul says to us, "Surely you know that Christ Jesus is in you" (2 Cor. 13:5). To simply be aware of these truths being spoken to us helps us to grow in faith.

There are many faith-building truths. As we listen to the word of the Lord, we will hear those truths being spoken to us. In fact, we can count on the Lord to repeat them to us and draw them to our attention as they grow dim in our minds. The more we live in the light of God's word, the more we will grow in faith.

PRAY FOR FAITH

The following suggestion is a simple, obvious one: we should pray for faith. That is a prayer that God always answers. We should persevere in that prayer until we see it happen within us, knowing that the Lord wants us to have faith and that he will give it to us. As it says in 1 John,

> "This is why we have courage in God's presence; we are sure that he will hear us if we ask him for anything that is according to his will. He hears us whenever we ask him; since we know this is true, we know also that he gives us what we ask from him."

(1 John 5:14-15)

We should, therefore, not pray for faith in a begging way, or in a way that acknowledges that we have no faith. We should pray for it by turning to Christ and remembering how much he wants us to have faith, and how he has given it to so many others in the past when they have turned to him for it.

BE WILLING TO TRY ACTING IN FAITH

When I first was prayed with for the gift of tongues, I was afraid to do anything at all that might be "me". I would not so much as move my lips, because I was afraid that I would be getting myself into praying in tongues. People worked to get me free from that fear, and after I was willing to try speaking in tongues, a change began to occur.

Once one of the attempts I made to speak in tongues was different from the others. There was a different ability to yield to the Spirit, a new spark of faith. If I had not been willing to try, I do not know what it would have taken for me to begin speaking in tongues.

The same lesson applies in more ordinary areas of our lives. We often do not relate to people in a good way, because we do not have the ability to do so, or at least we do not see that ability in ourselves. But once the Holy Spirit has been given to us, we have the source of the fruit of the Spirit inside us. We have a new power to relate to others in a successful way. One of the people I knew well in our community tended to be shy and had a difficulty being able to talk with people. He was afraid that they would not be interested in what he had to say, or, even worse, that he would not be able to think of anything to say. After a few months of his new life as a Christian, the Lord began to let him know that he had given him a new ability to relate to people and that as he tried using it he would see that it was there. He did try, and he could see something new happening. Today, he is able to talk freely with a wide variety of people and to serve and care for them in a responsible way.

God wants us to be unafraid. He expects us to learn to have faith, and he will give us faith. If we want to grow in faith for healing, we should pray with people to be healed, and pray for ourselves to be healed. If we do not have the faith to expect God to do things in a given area, we can at least trust him enough to expect him to increase our faith. We may even have to have the persistence of the man who went to his friend at night and demanded loaves of bread; we should be prepared to be that way, and not shrink back. We should not hold back until we feel perfect faith.

DO NOT TRY TO "WORK UP" FEELINGS OF FAITH, BUT LOOK TO THE LORD

Faith is a gift, not a feeling that we have to work up inside. I went through a period of "trying to have faith." I had noticed that at times of genuine faith, I often felt an assurance that God would act. And so when I tried to "have faith," I tried to produce that feeling of assurance inside of me. I would not pray for someone, or speak, or do anything until I had worked up a feeling of assurance. Well, it rarely seemed to work. It almost seemed, in fact, that the harder I tried to "have faith," the less it worked. Then I learned an important truth. I began to see that what I was doing was concentrating on myself. I was having faith in my feeling of assurance, rather than in Christ. I was beginning to think that if I felt a certain way, things would happen. But I also rediscovered another truth in the process — that trying to concentrate on having a certain feeling is often one of the worst ways of actually getting that feeling. The more I tried to produce a feeling of faith inside me, the harder it was for me to actually experience it.

We grow in faith, not by looking to ourselves, but by looking to Christ. What we need to focus on is not our own feelings (Christ often works despite them), but on him — on his power, on his promises, on what he has done in the past. What we need to fill our minds with and our hearts with when we try to act in faith or pray in faith is the Lord himself. As we turn to him, he will increase our faith.

PRAY FOR THINGS WITH CONFIDENCE

How we pray for things makes a big difference in our growth in faith. Often we have a tendency to beg God for things. Over and over we will ask him to give us what we want. The very approach of begging betrays a lack of faith. Whom do we beg but the person we do not believe will ever give us what we are asking for? God wants us to approach him confidently, as sons and daughters who are sure of their Father. When we ask, we should ask with confidence, thanking him for what he will do, confessing his power and Lordship, praising him. Our prayer should be an act of faith, not an indication of our lack of faith.

I once observed two acquaintances of mine who learned the same lesson, but in a different area. They were in love with one another, and the man had promised the woman that he would love her until he died. When she first heard him say it, she was happy. But she kept asking him over and over if he really would love her until he died. Finally one day they had a fight over the question, and he wanted to know if she had so little trust in him that she would never believe him when he said yes. She felt so insecure about herself that she could not believe him, He felt exasperated and hurt, because her constant asking made him feel that she did not think he could be trusted.

We do the same thing with God at times. We ask him as if he were not to be trusted, or as if he did not really love us. Sometimes we call his promises into question. It is true that what that shows is only that we are insecure. But we are treating him in a way that a human being would find insulting. We are praying to him as if we cannot expect him to help us, or sometimes as if he does not want to help us. That gets us into the kind of relationship with him in which it is harder for him to do things for us.

Our prayer is most effective when it is according to the truth. When we acknowledge that Jesus is the Lord and has all power in heaven and earth, when we call to mind his love for us and how much he wants to do for us, then we are beginning to pray in the Spirit of truth. The more our prayer is in the Spirit of truth, the more effective it is.

RESIST SPIRITS OF FEAR AND DOUBT

There are many things in us which work against faith: fears, doubts, hesitancies, confusions, anxieties. There is a great deal about the way we are which is an obstacle to growth in faith. But Peter tells us that we also have to be aware that we have to deal with evil spirits who work upon the natural things in us and stir them up, making it more difficult to have faith. Peter says,

> *"Throw all your worries on God, for he cares for you. Be alert, be on watch! For your enemy, the Devil, roams around like a*

*roaring lion, looking for someone to devour.
Be firm in your faith and resist him."*

(1 Pet. 5:7-9)

Paul tells us,

*"Put on all the armor that God gives you,
so that you will stand up against the Devil's
evil tricks. For we are not fighting against
human beings, but against the evil spiritual
forces in the heavenly world, the rulers,
authorities, and cosmic powers of this dark
age."*

(Eph. 6:11-12)

And James gives the simple advice to us,

"Oppose the Devil and he will flee from you."

(James 4:7)

One way in which evil spirits work upon us
is through lies. They begin to put thoughts into
our minds, thoughts which hinder our ability to
follow the Lord. They tell us, "it will never work"
or "you do not have enough faith" or "God will
never listen to someone like you" or "it didn't
work last time" or any number of different

thoughts. When we listen to those thoughts and believe them, our faith begins to drain away. Instead we have to resist them. We have to say to ourselves, "I know what the truth is, and those thoughts are not the truth." If we give in to all the thoughts of doubt and fear that go through our heads, we will not be able to grow in faith.

A big obstacle to our ability to resist the work of evil spirits is our tendency to live by our feelings. Many of us tend to approach situations with the idea, "if I feel that way, that's the way it must be." We think that if we feel we cannot do something, we cannot, or if we feel fearful, we have to act in a fearful way. But we do not have to follow our feelings. If we do follow our feelings evil spirits will have a field day with us, because they can more easily work on our emotions than any other aspect of us. The Holy Spirit gives us the ability to follow the Lord no matter how we feel. We have to claim that power and begin to act on it. We have to recall the truth and act in faith even when we are opposed by feelings of fear and doubt.

GO TO WHERE OUR FAITH CAN BE FED

If our faith is fed by seeing God act and by being in contact with committed Christians who have faith, we should go to situations in which we can see God act and where we can make contact with men and women of faith. If we want to grow in faith, it only makes sense to go where our faith will be helped. For most of us that means looking around for the nearest group of Christians who are beginning to experience a growth in faith and joining with them. It is difficult to grow in faith by ourselves.

Of course, we cannot always see God act when we want to (we could if we had the faith, the problem is often getting to the point of faith), nor can we always find a group of Christians who can help our faith. Or sometimes we are part of a group of Christians struggling to grow in faith, but the whole group needs help to grow in faith. Ten years ago, I would not have known how to get myself into a situation in which I could grow in faith the way I am able to now. In such a case books can be a great help. For me, it was the reading of *The Cross and the Switchblade* that revolutionized my faith. By reading a book on how God acted, my faith was fed, fed to the point where I could make a resolve to do whatever I had to do to grow into the kind of faith that I saw in the book.

Books, in fact, can often feed faith, and if we want to grow in faith, reading certain books can help us. *The Cross and the Switchblade* is one such book, as is *Realities*. *I Believe in Miracles* is another, as are *The Little Flowers of St. Francis of Assisi* and *The Miracles of Lourdes*. There are many books written about how God has acted in history that can make us see that what we read about in the Scriptures is not just something that happened in a Never-Never Land, nor in a special period of past history, but that has happened in every age since Christ and is happening today to people like us.